Cancer In Me!

FRANKIE

BALBOA.PRESS

A DIVISION OF HAY HOUSE

Balboa Press books may be ordered through booksellers or by contacting:

Balboa Press
A Division of Hay House
1663 Liberty Drive
Bloomington, IN 47403
www.balboapress.com.au
1 (877) 407-4847

Print information available on the last page.

ISBN: 978-1-5043-2033-7 (sc)
ISBN: 978-1-5043-2034-4 (e)

Balboa Press rev. date: 01/10/2020

Contents

Acknowledgements

I wish to thank June for her ongoing encouragement and support writing this book. Her knowledge, insight of writing and generosity with emotional support has been extremely helpful. June has recently had a baby, and everyone knows babies take up a lot of time, so I am grateful she made time to help me. I enjoy the early morning contact I have with my Mum, my sister and her four children. The regular chats and playfulness keep my spirits up. I also cannot forget my mother's Maltese Terrier, he such a comfort and support when I visit. I would also like to acknowledge Maree and her two children. Their unconditional love is a big part of my world.

To Louise and Silvia for their guidance, nurturing and genuine support. I appreciate the extra mile they go to care for me.

I am fortunate with the oncology staff, admin, nurses, doctors, volunteers at the Hospital for their emotional support and amazing care. I enjoy the humor and playfulness the nurses offer which makes my time at the hospital much more enjoyable. Their jobs go beyond the oncology unit with the extra care they provide with one nurse dropping in medication to me on his way home and another phoning to check on my mental state. There were also many volunteers making sure I was comfortable while going through treatment, providing food, drinks and blankets. I am touched by their genuine care. As I am with the care from the Medical Centre staff, my GP and the other doctors, nurses and admin staff- they have all been extremely supportive.

I was honoured having the ongoing support of my friends and through some very hard times in my treatment, they know who they are. One with her adventurous personality, generosity and with her lovely border collie. My most recent friend and her Jack Russel have also been an excellent support; we have weekly contact. The Jack Russel is so funny to watch; she is hyperactive and has energy in leaps and bounds chasing balls. While we are talking, she doesn't like being excluded, she craves attention.

The owners of the local cafe play a big part of my day. I purchase my coffee, have laughs jokes and banter. It keeps me on the go. If I need anything I feel I can always go there and they both encourage this.

To all the wildlife that visit, birds that come for a feed on my deck- Kookaburras', Magpies, Butcher Birds, Pigeons, Doves, Bush Turkeys and on the rare occasion King Parrots and Rosella's, thank you for making sure

I'm never lonely. This is a privilege to live in a lovely environment like I do, nature is important to me the creek across the road, plenty trees providing comfort and beautiful views.

Introduction

This is a true narrative about my own life living with cancer. I am the main character and the content is based on my treatments and the challenges I am confronted with while also touching on my will and determination to live.

The story discusses the concept that those in the community and in hospital talk about cancer as though it is automatically related to dying. It also expresses the dislike I feel when being spoken to like I'm in God's waiting room. The story centres around my diagnosis of Stage IV Metastatic Breast Cancer in 2017 and my refusal to just give up and die. Having a strong mind and positive self-talk are some of the techniques I will describe in the book that have assisted me to continue to live each day to the best of my ability. Like other illnesses people learn to live with I am just living with mine.

I also talk about how my past has influenced the determination I have today. Through self-reflection I have developed the strength needed to fight my cancer.

The aim of the book is to share my experiences with the hope to inspire and educate others that Cancer does not necessarily mean death. The audience I plan to target is people that need a positive view rather than a defeatist attitude about living with a terminal illness. This will be open to anyone that has either been diagnosed or is supporting a person with cancer.

Names and identifying details have been changed to protect the privacy of individuals.

Chapter One
Diagnosis

It was the eighth of February 2017, I was called into the Medical Centre to see my GP as they had received my results from my bone marrow biopsy. I was scared and aware that the news was not going to be good after weeks of having various tests and procedures and seeing several specialists. I was a sick woman with an extremely low white and red blood cell count. Feeling tired and cold most of the time, all I wanted to do was sleep.

The afternoon I attended my appointment but was not able to see my usual doctor. My GP was not working that day, so I was booked in to see her co-worker, who had to inform me that cancer cells had been found in my bone marrow. I burst into tears. The doctor admitted me to the nearby Hospital as he had seen just how urgently I needed a blood transfusion. I remember how pale I looked and how I was struggling to stand up. I spent the night at the hospital and was given some blood. The next day he had planned on giving me another dose, however after my GP had spoken with the Oncologist, I was transferred to a bigger hospital for more scans and tests.

On Thursday the ninth of February 2017 I was admitted again but this time the doctors seemed to have more knowledge of what they were looking for.

I had an ultrasound on my breast and ovaries, nothing seemed to show up. The next day I was sent for another ultrasound and while being examined, I noticed the Radiologist calling the doctor into the room, it was then I knew that they had found something.

Not long after returning to my room from the ultrasound my friends from work, Peter and Bec visited. I expressed to them the concerns with my ultrasound believing the doctors had found something. We were all waiting anxiously for the doctors, I was laying on the bed, Bec was sitting beside me, and Peter was standing at the end of my bed. There were also three other patients in the room with me. As I was waiting for the doctors, I was chatting with a young lady and her mother who were sitting across from me, they were dealing with their own health issues.

Eventually the time came to find out my diagnosis. Two doctors, one of them an intern and a nurse arrived. I remember the curtains being slowly drawn across for privacy. The Oncologist spoke with his gentle voice, he said a lump was found under my right breast close to the arm pit roughly 20cm diameter. I automatically shut down; I don't remember much that was said only that I was diagnosed with stage four metastatic breasts cancer.

I could see mouths moving but could hear no sound. I was in shock and struggled to speak. I started to cry. Peter and Bec attempted to comfort me at the same time holding back their own tears. I just laid on the bed staring at the ceiling for what felt like an eternity. The doctors eventually left and the mother of the young lady across from me approached and hugged me, she also reassured me that this will be a journey but I'm strong enough to get through it. She told me that I could apply to access my superannuation early so I could support myself financially while going through treatment. At the time I was not in the right headspace to fully comprehend what she was telling me. Shortly afterwards the nurses returned, and I was given another blood transfusion before being sent home with a stack of paperwork detailing my next steps and treatment.

Peter drove me home, on the way we stopped at the pharmacy to pick up the medication the doctor prescribed, while Peter was in the chemist, I had phoned mum sobbing and shared my news. I told mum I wanted no calls from my siblings as I needed time to digest the news myself.

That Friday evening, I had planned on getting pissed with my friends wiping myself out in hope of forgetting about the news I had recently received, only for my body to reject the beer. I became nauseas and my friends left earlier than expected apart from Peter who hung around until the next day.

Saturday I was on my own, drowning in my thoughts

and fear, wondering what was next for me. Am I going to die? Is it my time to go? and if so, why now, what was the point of my life?

I thought about the issues I was confronted with at work at the time, the challenges that I was faced with. I felt like I was being bullied and harassed standing up for myself. I also considered my own personal issues that I was challenged with and seeking support for. I had been seeing a therapist regularly and was working towards a healthier and more balanced life. But what was the point of all that if I was just going to die? The more I thought about it the angrier I became.

After several hours of going through the motions, from fear to anger, yelling at God, telling him I don't need any more challenges. I eventually grounded and found my strength and determination to fight for my life. I came to terms with the journey ahead of me and embraced the unknown. I am not afraid to die but I am not ready to go.

I thought about the many people being diagnosed with cancer and how it was common enough like seeing a flu going around. I had read and listened to people's inspiring stories of living beyond expectancy and I am determined to be one of these people.

Chapter Two
What Next?

The following week I had a platelet transfusion then a breast biopsy. I was injected with a local anaesthetic to numb my breast, then from the oncology unit I was wheeled in on the bed to radiology. As I entered, I noticed the radiologist at the ultrasound machine. I transferred onto the bed beside him. Within a short time, he inserted a needle hook into my breast which I watched on the screen above me. There were also students in the room watching while the doctor was explaining the process. I noticed the doctor was paying more attention to talking than watching what he was doing. The next minute I jumped and yelped as he missed the marked spot and got me in a place that was not numb. The pain brought tears to my eyes and I felt like punching him. Looking at the nurses faces they also looked like they wanted to pound him. I was so pissed off. I wanted to tell him to focus and stop flapping his gums, but I kept quiet.

Friday the 24th of February, I had my first appointment with the Professor at the hospital. This was my first consultation with an Oncologist since I was diagnosed.

I really liked the Doctor he was so gentle, compassionate and had a good sense of humour. He showed me on his computer screen my bone scan and where the cancer is. I remember seeing three spots in my vertebrae. He went through the scan thoroughly. I become overwhelmed and attempted to cut him off, he respectfully demanded that I pay attention and said it is important for me to understand the process and procedure. I took in what my next step was, which at the time was all I could deal with. I just wanted to start the treatment rather than dwell on the side effects and hear about treatment prolonging my life.

The Doctor examined my breast and mentioned the lump in my breast was more than the size of a fifty-cent piece and was bigger than first thought.

The plan of action was that I have chemotherapy to stop the cancer in motion and shrink the lump before they operated to remove it.

Tuesday the 28th of February 2017 I attended the group training and education day which was organised by the oncology nurses. There were many people with cancer there and the majority had already begun their treatment while some were going through their second and third rounds of chemotherapy.

I went alone to the group. I was encouraged to bring a support person and at the time my nieces and great niece were visiting, but I chose to go alone as I did not want them to worry, as keen as they were to come and support me.

I was given a lot of information on chemotherapy; the side effects, what I needed to be mindful of and what I could and could not do. There are certain foods I cannot eat, like shell fish. It was made clear that I had to be so careful to prevent infection of any sort. I was to avoid public places like shopping centres and swimming pools. This sucked for me considering swimming is one of the activities that I enjoy. I had to stay away from visitors and anyone who was sick, even people showing signs of a cold.

Keeping my own personal hygiene was also a high priority, considering radiation going through my body and the impact this may have on other people that are around me.

I became extremely overwhelmed with all this information and got upset, my world had turned upside down and I felt powerless. One of the brochure's I received in the group pissed me off, 'getting my affairs in order'. I thought "fuck that", my affairs involve living and that's where my focus is.

Straight after the training I had my first chemotherapy treatment. I went from one room to another. I was directed to a burnt orange chair, the nurse followed with her trolley. I was asked several questions, checking that I had administered the medication in the morning as directed by oncologists.

A canula was inserted into the veins of my arm, the nurse then prepared by putting on the safety equipment-coat, gloves and mask. Soon after the Abraxane chemo drug was administered I suffered a reaction; this was a terrifying experience. I went red and burned up. The nurses quickly stopped the machine and followed the medical procedure. Fear crept upon me as I stressed about the treatment not working. The staff must have seen the fear on my face as one of them reassured me that there are many other treatments if this failed. I was sent home with an increase of steroids to take and planned to return the next day to try again. Dosed up with the steroids my body accepted the treatment. Taking the steroids was not so good though as they had a negative impact on my sleeping pattern.

In March I had a chest port put in just above my right breast, it was a small procedure. A port is a small "medical appliance that is installed beneath the skin. A catheter connects the port to the vein. Drugs can be injected, and blood samples can be drawn many times without the discomfort of the needle stick". It was so much easier having this in. The port was soon tested as I had chemo straight after.

I had family come and go, some were supportive others were not so much, I wondered why they come at all.

My Sister was around at the beginning, she had transported me to the hospital a few times while she was visiting. One time we were waiting in the Emergency Department, I could barely stand never mind walk. I had little blood, I looked yellow and I felt nauseas. I went to the bathroom where I ended up laying on the floor for a short time and had to be supported back to the waiting room.

I continued to react having ups and downs with the chemo. During one session I got massive stomach pain and cramps and was running around hospital like a chook with its head chopped off. I ended up in the emergency. The next day I travelled to another hospital as the hospital I usually go to only does treatments on a Monday. I tried again and again I reacted. Third time lucky I thought, and I had an increase of steroids and I went back in on the Wednesday. Hooray it worked, and I was left buzzing from the high dose of steroids. For months I seemed to live at the hospital, having everything from blood transfusions, to high temperatures' and infections.

By the end of April, I started to settle and get into a routine. I didn't have much choice but to embrace the cancer as part of my life. Gradually, over time my intake of steroids decreased and having weekly chemo became the norm for me.

I have been fortunate with all the staff in the oncology unit. The compassion and warmth I experience from the nurses, admin staff and doctors has been phenomenal. I see myself as being blessed.

Chapter Three
Chemotherapy

In my experience there are twelve sessions of chemotherapy in a cycle and I had two cycles over seven months with a break in between. Having a break in the middle was due to me having a lumpectomy with my lump from my breast being removed. The chemo treatment had shrunk the lump. I had two operations on my breast, my surgeon was not happy with the first one. She was concerned that the margin was not scraped as well as she had hoped. I was away when the Doctor decided to go back in. A week after my first operation she phoned me while I was in Sydney for the weekend. As soon as I returned home I went straight in for the second procedure.

On my right breast I have a neat, now faded scar.

I heard many people share their thoughts on chemotherapy. Most of these thoughts were not something I needed to hear. People also shared their knowledge on natural treatments and encouraged me to try these rather than have chemotherapy. I am all for natural therapies and am accustomed to them, however this was not something I took lightly. This is my life and I need to do what is best for me. When I asked about their knowledge on the survival rate of these therapies very little was said.

It is not in my nature just to give up, I am a determined and feisty woman with a strong will. In saying this, as much as I am a fighter and focus on being positive I am challenged with my health.

I pray, asked for guidance and I go with my gut. I put faith in my doctors considering they are the ones that have studied many years, and this is their field of expertise. I acknowledge chemotherapy is not nice however it works and that is something I'm going with.

Chemotherapy felt like having a bad taste in the mouth, but this is a bad taste in your whole body that you cannot easily be rid of. It feels unhealthy and inhumane. The side effects, metallic taste, the foggy brain, and the nausea all came at once.

With my foggy brain I struggled to explain my thoughts and put them into words. Day dreaming is the best description, drifting in and out like a shadow in the world.

At times going to bed I was a little scared and wondered if I would wake up. My head got so hot sometimes that I had to put a cold pack behind my neck to feel some sort of relief. My back also ached.

Losing my hair for the first time was a shock, I went into shame, feeling yuck within and looking at myself in the mirror, only seeing my pale-yellow face with dark eyes and no hair. Not an attractive look but lucky for me I only felt this way for a short time. I eventually detached from my image/ego.

I struggled to find ways to balance my life, living it to its fullest each day while in treatment. My way of thinking is that I am fighting for my life but what was the point if I was just laying down sleeping. Knowing myself I knew this was not good for me either. I am also aware of my need to find a balance that serves my well-being and works alongside my treatment. Experimenting with cannabis oil supported me, prevented nausea and increased my appetite. I pushed myself to do what I took for granted and in the past would do automatically, such as getting up, having a shower and getting dressed. These simple things were not so simple anymore, sitting up for a short time was a big day for me. With constant self-talk I got up and began doing a little more each day. My days may consist of spending time in my garden, sitting on the veranda and enjoying the sunshine, having coffee at the local café. Sometimes with my friends and family I would go for a drive and take a short walk on the beach.

Limited in what I'm able to do I returned to reading biographies and one author got my attention and inspired me to keep going, it also confirmed my belief of the other side. "Die to be me" by Anita Moorjana had me feeling empowered and believing that anything is possible, even miracles. I believe if I'm meant to go from this world it's out of my control so the best thing I can do for myself is to live and just get on with it.

Chapter Four
Reflection

Having cancer is a life changer and has deeply moved me to focus on matters of the heart. I began to question how I got here and what cancer means to me. I refused to see cancer as a death sentence and am more inclined to see this as a rebirth process, a time to slow down and heal my body on all levels.

I had to separate families and friends fears from mine. As much as I have a strong mind this was not always easy to do. People's fears and thoughts were confronting. I was often spoken to like I was in gods waiting room and on my death bed and this challenged my thinking. At times I became overwhelmed with others defeatist attitude towards my cancer.

I remember my dentists' attitude. I had to have dental work done before I was able to get the denosumab injection, something to do with calcium. While at the preparation appointment my dentist blurted out and said if I was going to die there is no point wasting my money in having the wisdom teeth taken out. I was speechless. I thought seriously, do you really think I would be here? I don't plan on dying you're heartless fuck.

I have been in treatment now going on three years. The hormonal tablets stabilized the cancer in my bone marrow for nineteen months.

Early in 2019 I started to feel discomfort in my stomach and oesophagus which was out of the ordinary for me. My Doctor referred me for an endoscopy and colonoscopy procedure where they took a biopsy. Again, I was called in to get the results. I remember driving home from my therapy session, the doctor phoned and asked me to come in as soon as possible. I was about 30 minutes out from the medical centre. I sobbed all the way to the clinic. I sat in the car park for a while trying to wipe the tears. I felt highly vulnerable, but I finally got the courage to go into the building. The tears kept falling out of my control and continued while seeing the doctor. One of the admin staff comforted and hugged me. The staff are always a pleasure to see, this day was no different. The results showed that I had cancer in my stomach. I was then sent for a PET scan which picked up spots on my ovaries and I returned to chemotherapy.

I believe that the cancer found in my stomach has been there all along, before I was diagnosed, I was having problems in my stomach but then the cancer took my attention and I did not think about it. At the time chemo was working, its only when I was put onto the hormonal tablets that my stomach inflamed. The doctor informed me the hormonal tablets don't work for the stomach cancer that's why we changed medications. Anyway, it is what it is.

I completed another round then the oncologists changed my medication to oral chemo that only came out 2018- KISQALI 200mg. I'm also on a new hormonal tablet APO-LETROZOLE 2.5MG I administer both each day at home.

This time round it was more challenging to maintain my resilience, with compounding physical side effects and emotional and mental ones as well. For a short time, I lost sight and I did not see the point with plans and goals for the future. I thought this may be my time up. What supported this was opinions from media and the public.

People seemed to be inclined to go out of their way to share stories of someone they knew who had cancer and died. Unbeknownst to them their timing was way out. I thought thank god I'm not you I would be dead already. The negativity people carry, I could not get away from. I turn the Television on there is someone telling their story of cancer and on a music show "the voice" I said loudly at the TV "fuck off with the cancer". Then there are the cancer ads which also became overpowering and all too much. I just wanted a break.

I eventually became grounded and realized I cannot change the way others think. I cannot control what goes on TV. I can choose what I take on board and how I move through this without the extra stress from other opinions and fears. To stay focused I often challenged my own thinking, when I'm feeling flat, I check in with myself by asking a range of questions. I explore my feelings and thoughts. Looking within and being aware of the side effects from my medication supports me to do something active to move the energy. I swim, kayak, walk or I ride my bike.

I have a couple of strategies I do to stay focused and keep positive. I reminisce what a man from the local café once said to me. He also has cancer and shared with me a Charlie Brown and Snoopy quote. Charlie brown said to Snoopy "Someday we will die", Snoopy replied "True, but on all the other days we will not".

I also say a prayer each day that my mum shared with me-

A prayer for today!

"Every day I need you lord, but this day especially.
I need some extra strength to face whatever is to be.
This day more than any day I need to feel you near,
to fortify my courage and to overcome my fear.
By myself I cannot meet the challenge of the hour there are times when human creatures need a higher power. to help them bear what must be born
And so dear lord, I pray hold on to my trembling hand and be with me today."

One of the major lessons for me that I continue to grapple with is slowing down. I was not aware how much I rushed through my life until I got sick. I rushed that much I missed myself, my needs and having no care for my wellbeing.

Cancer put a pause on my life and I had no choice but to change pace, from being active to inactive and this is a process on its own. Laying on my bed left in silence with only my thoughts, I began to look at myself in a way I had not done before. I started to listen to my body, hear my breathing, feel my aches and pains. I share my feelings and thoughts with my therapist who I regular see. All the above supports me to reconnect and see myself in a new light.

I acknowledge I lived to work, If I was not working with my co-workers, I was drinking with them and getting pissed. A negative routine that I struggled to move away from.

Deep down I yearned for change. I wanted something much more meaningful, I did not know how to go about getting this and I was not sure what I wanted.

There were times I attempted to change my ways. I enrolled in TAFE courses to retrain in something different however my work environment made this difficult for me to complete. The work politics drained the goodness out of me, leaving me having little energy. I gather I gave up to some degree.

I often think of the tortoise and the hare story, I use this as a healing tool. The hare rushing was me in the past and the tortoise strolling in a leisurely way enjoying the scenery is more me now.

I understand the importance of living in my integrity, doing things in my own timing, and for my own well-being. One of the biggest lessons I have learned is gentleness, being gentle with myself.

I have good friends that support me, and I catch up with regularly. I focus on being useful and partaking in activities I can do that will get me through the day. I have a balance of activity and rest. Most importantly I stay positive, I avoid taking on other people's thoughts and beliefs. For me living is healing.

I don't live close to my family and when necessary I rely on my friends. I am lucky to have good mates. At the beginning Peter was one who supported and transported me to my appointments. He saw the impact cancer had on me and experienced the frustrating health system. It took a long time for the doctors to know what was wrong with me.I was in and out of the hospital's emergency department and the medical center where I see my GP (General Practitioner). One time I was referred to a liver specialist. I remember the night before my appointment, I struggled to sleep, feeling highly unsettled and so agitated that I couldn't relax, my body in pain. The next morning Peter had to take me to the local hospital to get pain killers before being transported comfortably to see the specialist, which was over an hour away. In the waiting room I could not stand up for long and I ended laying on the floor, I did not care how it looked, I was so sick. I had a chest and liver scan, and both came back clear. The specialist expressed her sympathy as she told me there was nothing more she could do and yet again I was sent home.

The process of finding out what was wrong with me seemed a long and winding road. My GP was good though, she did not give up and she asked for help outside of her expertise. I ended up seeing haematologist and he admitted me to the hospital for more tests but under another specialist as he went away. Most of these specialists were interns that seemed to have big egos. After a few days they sent me home writing my illness off as the side effects of homeopathic medicines. This left a bad taste in my mouth. I was shocked, so I acted and wrote a complaint to the Doctor who admitted me. Here I was head on pillow, knees bent, laptop on them and I was typing on an angle. I was sick, and my anger supported me to push through with my complaint.

I felt that I was put at risk by the doctors sending me home, considering I could not walk too far, my bloods were abnormal, and I live alone. Lucky for me the complaint got the ball rolling and I got the support I desperately needed. I see how the health system is no different from life, just waiting for change to happen does not always go to plan or to expectation. At times you must fight for what is right and in this case it's my health and life.

Chapter Five
Unfinished business

My unfinished business is dealing with my past and family. I am a changed woman since seeking support. By asking for support in dealing with my past I learned important skills to process and live with my cancer diagnosis. Facing my issues has made me a stronger person. Living with cancer I rely on this strength each day.

I grew up in a large family. I am one of nine children, number seven, the third youngest. I acknowledge my mother having two miscarriages they were before my time.

There was a lot of yelling, screaming and fighting between siblings growing up. Dad was an electrician however he could not maintain a job for long periods and was home a lot looking after us while mum worked. Most of the family time was dysfunctional and kept secret. Dad wiped himself out by over medicating with his medication. He took more pills than he was prescribed. When he was not off his face, locked in his room, he was not always a nice person. What us kids all had in common was to protect ourselves from dad. I remember my elder siblings stuffing pillows under my clothing to protect me from the jug cord we got hit with. When or if we misbehaved, he would get us to stand beside each other in a line and one by one, no-one missed out from the cord. He did not seem to notice how big our bodies were when we hid pillows underneath our clothes but there were times, we had no time to prepare and I was left with welt marks on my legs.

Mum had her hands full looking after eight children. My younger sister was born much later, so I was often missed and unprotected. My elder siblings were not supportive, they were surviving their own way. Our family was more competitive for attention than supportive which Dad encouraged. The violence and aggressive behaviour became normal in the household. When my brothers were hitting each other, Dad yelled at them to get outside and have a good old Donny brook which meant punch up in slang terms.

I was often accused of being Dad's favourite because he allowed me to stay up longer than my elder siblings to watch the Rugby league. I loved Parramatta eels. Dad also took me to the neighbours without mum knowing, just few houses down the street to one of his close friends who we treated as an uncle. I don't remember a lot being there only that they drank alcohol. I do recall mum sending one of my sisters or brothers to come and get me to bring me home. This created another reason for my siblings to pick on and bully me. Though I did not make things easier for myself. I annoyed and tormented my sisters as we all shared a room. There was a single bed and a set of bunks in the room, I was on the bottom bunk. I would always push the top bunk with my feet, it pissed my sister off. One time I pushed the bed and it came out of its socket. The bed collapsed onto me with my sister on it, my legs were holding it up. I screamed for mum and to this day my sister and I laugh about, though it wasn't as funny at the time.

Another memory I have is of a cupboard between our beds. I continuously kicked the door tormenting two of my sisters while they were trying to sleep. They got me back telling me scary stories about the boogie man standing at the window coming to get me, this scared the shit out of me.

Going to sleep was a struggle, I was restless and once I got to sleep, I was often disturbed with nightmares, talking and yelling and grinding my teeth. I even attempted to climb the wall while I was sleeping, I was told what I did the next day by mum or my sisters. I have memories of being frightened of the dark and screaming out to mum to come and take me to the toilet. Many times, in distress I attempted to yell but struggled to make a sound, I could only gasp. I kept trying until I made noise and mum came in. One experience I never forgot is yelling out for mum to take me to the toilet, when I returned and jumped back into bed I screamed in fear, it was like I jumped into somebody's body, it was evil.

I went through a stage of listening to the radio while in bed, I could not sleep without it, back then there was a talk back radio station called sounds of silence hosted by Father Jim McLaren, to me he was Father Jim, a man who allowed his guest to share their stories and problems while he attempted to offer advice and assist with addressing their issues and praying for them. At a young age I was interested in people's problems. I can recall laying on my bed listening to what people were sharing, I heard nothing else, all the noise of the household diminished. I remember feeling sad when individuals got upset while talking and many of the stories touched me deeply. I can remember praying for my own life, not wanting to have children so they didn't end up going through what I was at the time.

The family communication was through alcohol, sometimes it was good and other times it was a nightmare. A family get together often ended in violence. My brothers would often drink too much and go looking for a fight, lashing out at anyone. Through my own usage of alcohol and aggression, I reacted verbally and ended up being hurt by them. No- one protected me. I got to the point after being hit so much, I thought I may as well stand my ground and fight back I get hit anyway.

I started martial arts to protect myself from my brothers and at the beginning it was for revenge. My thoughts were "you hit me again and I will break your knee caps". I was disciplined in my training I learned a lot and connected with myself on a physical level. I became confident in defending myself. By training and studying martial arts I calmed down a lot and my thinking changed. I no longer attended martial arts for revenge, it became a healthy outlet for me. I remember hearing the words from a Steven Siegel movie, "easy to hurt someone than to heal" and this stuck in my mind, I did not want to hurt anyone.

Moving away from family was the best thing I did for myself as hard as this was. I desperately wanted and needed something much more than my past had to offer. I yearned for so much more in my life. I remember telling myself there must be something better than what I am doing. Fortunately for me moving away paid off in more ways than one. I am my own person, standing in my integrity, not accepting negative influences, opinions or judgments. I feel free. Moving on from my past and dealing with the negative emotions that came from it is what has allowed me to build strength and fight my cancer. By getting to know myself and what I can deal with I have been able push through my cancer diagnosis and the difficulties that have come with it.

Chapter Six
Seeking support

I have been in therapy with Louise going on four years with breaks in between. Louise is my main support considering I live alone and have no partner to confide in. I share a lot with her.

I am usually a private person and I don't like many people knowing my business. Since seeking support, I have noticed a huge change in myself. I am much more content and open with myself. This has made a big deal in my relationships and contact with the world.

I was referred to Louise by another therapist Silvia who I had been seeing when I lived on the Sunshine coast. Silvia is a Gestalt therapist and I met her in my first year of training to be a Gestalt therapist. I learned a lot from Silvia and one of her teachings I took on board. The importance of the breath which I refer to as the voice of the body. In my sadness Silvia reminded me to focus on my breathing which supported me to move through the waves of emotion. Deep breaths into the body, breathing in through the nose and longer breaths breathing out through the mouth and at a pace that suits me.

At first my breathing was fast but after doing this a few times, I felt much calmer within. Actively participating in these breathing exercises, I got to feel in my body where my blockages are. This become a powerful and therapeutic tool to slow down as is sitting in the silence and listening to myself.

Louise is also a gestalt therapist and social worker; the work we do together continues from the work I did with Silvia. My health issues are just part of the everything else, neither I nor Louise put an emphasis on it, unless I need to go here.

Talking about my issues with another person each week has made a difference in my personal growth. I notice when I'm in a deep process no matter how difficult, I come out the other end feeling much more grounded and empowered. I am working more from my adult self. This supports me with enhancing my coping mechanisms to deal with health issues.

Before therapy I was stagnant in my life. I was not moving much at all just going around in circles, drifting from one place to another. I had no idea what happiness truly was or how to get this. I repressed my feelings, thoughts, pain and sadness down into my body which eventually impacted my well-being on all levels. My body was gasping for breath, I became overweight, eating the wrong foods, self-medicating with alcohol and the outcome was that I grew further apart from myself and became aloof.

Throughout my life I struggled with depression and anxiety, not that I was ever diagnosed but I experienced this strongly and my daily life was often difficult as a result. I lived in a space that was far from reality. I could never really explain my experiences, only imagine that they didn't happen. I relate my past self to a baby put in the desert to survive on its own. The stress I went through and what my body has gone through, I'm not surprised I have cancer. I do believe stress is one of the factors that has triggered Cancer in me.

I often have discussions with Louise about constantly feeling between worlds and not really understanding my experience. I share with her what it's like for me. I'm here but don't feel fully present in the moment, like I'm in a day dream.

I thought this may be related to my spiritual path, but over time Louise enlightened me about how my experience may also have been caused from the impact of past trauma.

I thought about this a lot and can see how my issues of depression and disconnection, contribute to my feeling between worlds. I imagine my repressed issues squashing into my body, choking the natural flow and separating the connection between my mind, body and soul which only invites in the darkness and depression. Dealing with my inner world of darkness through simple breathing strategies, placing focus in my body and seeking support from Louise, I am gradually shedding light to these places.

Louise is a therapist that focuses on self-regulating and works towards empowering the client. She is also a shiatsu practitioner and often shares her knowledge. We experiment with other natural therapies, guided meditation techniques and Energy focused tapping (EFT). The tapping of my body shifts the negative energy, we tap the many points in our bodies while talking. This is a powerful and supportive practice. Keeping the body and mind calm makes my life so much more functional. lightens my load and allows energy to flow much more freely.

The natural therapies are nurturing and support my recovery.

This balances the doom and gloom of living with Cancer.

Chapter Seven

Death/ The other side

Death to me is not a scary place, I grew up believing in the other side.

I remember my grandmothers, My father's mother was a strict Christian and attended church weekly. When she stayed over, us kids had to go to Sunday school, and I was not keen as it took me away from playing with my friends and it was embarrassing. We were always given an earful on what we could not do while we were at the church. One thing I remember we were not to accept food when offered. That sucked for a kid especially when there were sweet treats.

My mums' mother, a medium communicated with dead people, although she never called herself that. As a kid I remember visits from Nan and the adults fussing over her encouraging her to rest. My siblings and I were told Nan had a turn which I thought at the time related to a medical condition, that she was sick. As I got older, I understood she was having interactions with the dead that drained her energy and she become fatigued. I acknowledge the times she got so scared after receiving messages of someone passing over. which was confirmed true within a short time.

In my family we have a strong belief in the other side. My mum is intuitive, she has also had many communications with the dead. Mum has experiences of seeing, hearing and feeling the spooks around. When I go to her place, I feel them and it's like a morgue at times, so cold. The other side in our family is a playful joke, when I check in with mum and ask her has she had any visitors, she will tell me who had been around from both sides, dead and alive.

I have my own experiences; I feel a presence often and more than one. I know when I'm receiving healing/support from the other side. I get signs and messages through my dreams, and it's not in my head. I have worked with both settings being in therapy working through my past traumas and my spirituality, I know the difference and I acknowledge at times there is a fine line between the two.

My first book I read was Doris stokes who was an English medium, she had passed away many years before I knew who she was. I was fascinated by her world and work, reading about all the people she supported through her messages from the other side. I wanted to be a medium. Reading Doris' books were like sitting in the lounge room in front of the fire with a cup of tea talking with her.

Margaret Dent, I thought is the Australian version of Medium Doris stokes. I attended one of Margaret workshops at Ryde RSL club in NSW. Margaret made regular public appearances in clubs and entertain groups of people. She relayed messages from relatives and friends that have passed over to the other side. She was amazing!

My Mother and brother also attended the workshop with me. Margaret approached my mother and shared lyrics of a song. Unbeknownst to Margret they were words to a song my grandmother sang to my mother 'Alice blue gown' by Edith Day. My brother was also given a message from my grandfather to look after himself better. Believing in the other side is a huge support in my life. Reading about people's experiences inspires and supports me with my own challenges. Having faith and hope I believe anything is possible. I know when I lose my faith I fall hard.

Death is part of living, we go through rebirth cycles all the time. We all must face difficult challenges at least once in our lives. I see my illness as just this. Getting rid of the old and rebuilding the new me. Life is what you make of it. These days I am finding how amazing I can be, opening to my creativity. I am doing this by living each day, my way.

My Nephew died unexpectedly on Saturday seventh of December 2019 at age thirty. He was a young family man, loved his little girl, wife and life.

His death is sad and yet an awakening for me to appreciate life and live each day like it is my last.

Conclusion

I acknowledge life is what I make of it, whatever the challenges I am confronted with I have choice in how I react, respond and deal with the issue. I found having a choice is empowering to my well-being. I choose to surrender and work with my illness rather than fight, be angry and get myself all worked up. At times I dance between the two.

Finding my inner strength is the key to moving beyond the expectations, opinions and fears from others about having cancer.